The

JOY

of

ASCENSION

by

Randall Weischedel

Library of Congress Catalog Card Number: 82-073249

First Paperback Edition, 1987
ISBN: 0-87516-587-7

DeVorss & Company, Publisher
Box 550 – Marina del Rey, California 90294-0550

Printed in the United States of America

Acknowledgments

I wish to acknowledge first and foremost an entity called Ramtha the Enlightened One. He is an ascended master—in fact he was the first ascended master. That is to say, he was the first man born of the loins of man and womb of woman on this earth, or Terra as he calls it, to elevate his physical body into the realm of pure thought, or Spirit. Ramtha has been ever near this plane and teaches many of us to this day. He is committed, through his unspeakable Love, to our growth and our joy, and freedom from limitation. I have learned so much from Ramtha that it's difficult to separate Ramtha from Randall in my thoughts and in my knowingness, and so I have learned not to separate. Ramtha rescued me and returned me to my Self. Most of what I know is due to the doors which he assisted me to open. Ramtha is unlimited in his scope, and but a thought will reach him and draw him to you. If you desire his help, merely ask. As with all masters on all planes, you'll have much assistance.

Two other entities, Yeshua ben Joseph (you know him as Jesus of Nazareth) and Solano, are forever near and beloved of my Being. They have blessed me with their ceaseless Love and assistance, and encouragement that is beyond measure or description. My Love for these entities is unspeakable.

From the Lord God of my Being to the Lord God of your Being, dear reader, I dedicate this book. And to the Father that lies within me, without which I am nothing. To the God I Am. To the Christ Principle which I embody, and to ALL who proclaim themselves likewise.

There is nothing but water in the holy pools.

I know, I have been swimming in them.

All the gods sculpted of wood or ivory can't say a
word.

I know, I have been crying out to them.

The Sacred Books of the East are nothing but
words.

I looked through their covers one day sideways.

What Kabir talks of is only what he has lived
through.

If you have not lived through something, it is not
true.

> —by the fifteenth-century Indian poet
> Kabir

—taken from *The Kabir Book*, versions by Robert Bly
A Seventies Press Book, Beacon Press—Boston
Copyright © 1971, 1977 by Robert Bly .
Copyright © 1977 by The Seventies Press

Contents

The Joy of Ascension

As I contemplate my Being, the mind, the body, my emotions and impressions of all that is in Life, I realize how vast, how infinite Life is, how infinite God is. The first thing I must say about divine ascension, and this book in particular, is that to ascend the body is to *become* Life. There is no "path," no tricks will take you there. No one has a formula for ascension, and there are as many ways of doing it as there are Gods (people) in this universe and in all the universes. Ascension is accomplished in the moment you hold an experience, or a feeling, or a memory—which is a feeling—in your thought, in your Soul, which raises the bodily vibrations and, in short, makes you *feel good*. Any time you allow yourself to feel good about you, you expand within your auric structure, and eventually this expansion will lift your body right into a light principle, and you'll ascend.

If the contemplation of a silvery leaf in the spring rain as it skips and flits about is the joy and perfect image of that moment, then *feeling* it, cherishing it in your breast will open the doors to more understanding and *more* joy, more peace within you in your moments to follow. This is ascension and it leads most assuredly to LIFE, to eternal expression of the Self.

Life is really eternal for all, but most don't realize it and so live in fear of it, or worry about it ending or paining them or being just plain bad, and so it is. Each man is the lawgiver unto his own Being, and the attitude is the creator of all reality. For most Gods on this plane death is a certainty, for they worship it and believe in it and thus *know* it to be so. But to attain the seventh, which is to ascend the body, to take it with you, is so simple. It is truly simpler than death.

To ascend is merely to remove the fear and anxiety, the tension and turmoil, the limitations and definitions of Self, and to replace these with Love for Self, joy and freedom and purposeful intent in all your moments. This allows PEACE in the Being, and leads to the eventual and assured ascension of the body itself.

There is no method to ascending the flesh. Rather it is the natural result of *surrendering* the body to the wisdom of the Self, and simply *allowing* this transfiguration to occur.

I say simple, and herein lies the key. All that you have been conditioned to believe, and which this fabric, this web of social structure on this plane pulls you with great seductive power and constancy into, these are the illusory complexities and intricacies of a life where you are defined and circumscribed by that which the spokesmen for the masses have thus far allowed and approved as being "reality." Why, science is with every new day exploding the myths and superstitions that still hold sway in popular thinking. Each day the nature of this reality is being proved to be other than what it was known to be for ere so long on this plane. The illusions of this plane are very powerful. The struggle to overcome them is often arduous and painful. That is why a simplicity of perspective is so difficult here.

I have been through the fire, which is the reckoning of my own altered and cloistered attitudes. I have struggled and strived and all at my own hands, to overcome the limitations which I had assumed. When I was a little boy, I remember lying in the tall grasses watching the sun play with the clouds, and thinking: "What if I'm an amnesiac?

What if this is not really my house, my family, my "real" Life?" I remember that I *knew* that this was not my beginnings. This was not all that I was. And this is exactly the case. All who incarnate on this plane do so by agreeing to forget. When a child comes through the birth canal, the Soul enters the body and the entity forgets that which he has known beyond this world, and that which he has experienced in past expressions on this very plane. This allows the child-God to begin again fresh, and not to be at the mercy of old memories and details which often carry guilt and limitations above all else. This amnesia is encouraged as the child learns of "reality," and the memory is further *educated out* of him as he grows in an acceptable and fashionable pattern.

But I had not forgotten everything, and my Life has been a constant battle with my own alter-ego. I struggled arduously to fit in here, to find a concept of my "place" within a society that is too narrow and confining to contain my perceptions. All of you battle this same collective consciousness, this all-powerful "society." It is imageless and it is self-imposed. Fashion is placed above feelings here, and few find themselves comfortable in it, yet all wish to be accepted.

At last I learned to accept myself for what I Am. In this I learned that I sprang from the Mind of the

Father and am beholden to no outside force or entity for my Being, I simply and eternally AM. In my moments since that revelation, I have experienced sublime peace. I have also suffered many moments of painful searching and wrestling with Self to discover what Is-ness means and feels like. But in *all* my moments I have held steadfast to JOY, even the most tedious ones, for I see through this plane and recognize it for the great game that it is.

Thus, I express my deepest and heartfelt knowingness to you in this regard: the *simpler* I become in my pleasures and perception of this plane and its wonder, the grander and brighter my vision unfolds. The more of my Self I become, the lighter and more into Spirit the body becomes.

I have experienced the seventh. It is a Oneness with the Father, which is my own Spirit, and it is indescribable save to call it Is-ness.

I have flown through the air while the body sat on a stump or lay in my bed. I have known the exhilaration of limitlessness, complete freedom. And not freedom in ignorance, but freedom in Knowingness, moving across the skies and through space to wherever the thought takes me. It happens in an instant. When you take your consciousness (which is only perspective) from the body, it goes with the Spirit of your Being, and you are pure Thought, and in Thought there is no time or measure.

I have seen eternity stretch before my Eye, that I could taste its sweet clarity and feel its laughable simplicity in every pore, each fiber and particle of my Being. Other moments I am firmly rooted to the earth, seated by the shore and left to contemplate *this* plane and its magnificent beauty.

I have seen my body glow with luminescent light. For moments it will shimmer, then disappear to my eyes as I become One with the Spirit of all that surrounds me. In the next moment I am quite perceptibly of and on this plane, but I am learning to take the body with me, and it will never die.

I have conceived of, felt, and known limitless-ness, and I carry it in my Soul always, for it is this *feeling* which takes me into forever. As these moments occur more frequently and with greater clarity, I am inspired into this grand realization:
          This plane is the seventh.
I have become it, for I live it here. This is my con-clusive Is-ness reality, it is *HERE and NOW*.

Of all that I have perceived in an expanded totality,   anyone   can   perceive   such   things *immediately* in a moment of opening to the possibility. It is only the ones who need you as a "follower" that will tell you there are "steps" or rituals or dogmatic practices to be observed. They will not tell you that you are God. These other trappings of "spiritualism" are taught instead in order to keep a great people in a state of ignorance. For what would all these great "teachers" be with no one to follow them? None of these things are necessary. To arrive at the PEACE which will allow unlimitedness to be perceived, this is the difficulty here, for it requires patience and *Love of Self*. Few on this plane teach this, for it means that you must ponder and listen to and Love *YOU*, and then you would realize that you need no one, and you would be utterly free and totally unpredictable.

The fire of Self-awareness is sometimes hot, but no one receives anything that they aren't ready to handle. It is worth everything when the smoke settles and you can see yourself clearly again at long last. I, who have struggled much, will tell you, the struggle is only a game, an illusion. It is a powerful one, but in relation to your eternal beauty and ongoing Is-ness Self, it is but a moment in forever. Do not strive to be God-like. What *isn't* God-like when all things are of the Father? All that you are is *already* God, no thing is outside of the Father. Simply *BE*. All that is asked of you by the Father—

which is right within you in His completeness—is that you LOVE you, be YOU, enJOY you.

*   *   *

And so, dear friend, this book about divine ascension is about NOW, and not some future time or action that has not even arrived, for that is only conjecture. It is about living in *freedom of expression*, and Loving *you*. It is about my own impressions of the moments—which I call Life—and the ever greater understanding and compassion that I have for myself.

Love, as with all things, begins within. One must experience it with Self before one can express it to another. Of this which I tell you, it is not theory or philosophy, but LIFE which I've experienced and worship and live and see in a moment to moment awareness of that which is the *I AM that I AM.*

That which is beyond the visible and behind the physical world is not complex or esoteric, as so many would have you believe. And no dogma will ever replace your free will, or encompass the simple infinitude of the Father Principle. Its essence is completely understandable by *all*. My intent is to express this as concisely and clearly as written script will allow.

Words are only the symbols that have been agreed upon in order to share a thought and a feeling between us, but they are an incomplete substitute for the emotions that come from the experiences, which is called wisdom. And so, all that I have written and re-written in search for an expression of *exactness*, seems inadequate in expressing these feelings, which is Knowingness, that I wish to communicate to you. Still, I have chosen my words evenly and carefully, and would accept all of them back again in a century, for they represent me, they ARE me, and I Love this that I've written.

I do not ask you, dear reader, to *believe* anything that you read herein. I only ask that you read with the understanding that my expression leads to and from *feelings* and not intellect. The contemplation of these feelings, should you desire to, involves the intellect only as a tool, a door if you will, to a greater understanding and greater peace wherein "understanding" is not even required. This is the feeling of Is-ness and the seat of the Soul. Never is the intellect an end in itself, it is empty when it stands alone. It is *pure emotion* and *unaltered reason wedded* that lead to the kingdom of Heaven within you.

I ask you only to *feel* my words within yourself. If my unique perspective and humble learning can lift you in your esteem of Self for but a single moment, and allow you to consider a greater Love for YOU, then I am most successful and totally fulfilled in my Being. If you are not ready to Love yourself, to accept the premise that you created you, and all that you are involved in, then this little book may be difficult. If you are ready, then I desire that my straightaway Knowingness that God IS me, and YOU, and ALL PEOPLES, will inspire you to a higher and deeper arena of contemplative thought regarding the God that you BE.

From the first moment I heard Ramtha's name, all I wanted was to ascend. All I wanted was to BE Ramtha. A friend told me about him, that she had been to an audience with him several times and that he is an unlimited and completely enlightened God. What does that mean? She said that Ramtha lived on this plane thirty-five thousand years ago, in the last hundred years of Atlantis, and that he had never died. There is a remarkable woman named J. Z. Burnett who was his daughter then and serves as the channel for Ramtha. He is the only entity of the seventh plane that I'd ever heard of who comes through an individual of this plane. I went home that night floating six inches above the ground, and all I could think of was this Ramtha entity... Ramtha... Ramtha... RAMTHA...

I didn't sleep for three days, his name and his energy swirled in my consciousness. I felt his constant presence and unconditional Love for me. I heard his words and felt like he was inside of me. It felt as though he *was* me. My body began to change in a myriad of ways. The head throbbed, the pulse raced and my heart pounded into my throat and behind my eyes. My Soul felt as though it was moving around in my chest, and caused a queasy almost nauseating feeling.

A few weeks later I experienced my first "dialogue" with Ramtha speaking through J. Z.'s body. This beautiful, simple and gracious woman entered the room, was introduced as J. Z., the channel, and explained why she was there. She told how Ramtha had appeared to her and her husband, and began teaching them and their two sons. She explained that Ramtha has a body, which he ascended, and can bring it onto this plane into mass and form anytime he chooses. He has appeared to other individuals as well, but Ramtha does not appear to public audiences because he would be worshipped. He chooses this mode so that people have no image of him, no picture of what an ascended master should look like. In this way, he teaches that all must become their own ideal for themselves. This is the Ram's first message to this plane: The Father is within you. The ideal for you *IS* you, and cannot be found outside of yourself. All wisdom comes from within.

J. Z. went on to explain that unlike other mediums or channels, she actually leaves her body completely, Soul and all. She has no influence over or perception of the words and actions that come forth from her body when Ramtha comes through. She has no memory of what takes place during the dialogues. Ramtha takes her essence to a safe place, and is in total control of her Being during this time, for she has agreed to do this and allows it to occur. She abdicates her body so that none of what she feels or perceives will inhibit Ramtha's perspective. Ramtha has contemplated this plane for nigh a long time, and is unlimited in his understanding and Love and evenness. He is able to assess any attitude or problem without any judgment whatsoever, and he compares you to no one.

My dialogues with this entity have enriched my life beyond measure or description, but the greatest learning has been in my communication with Ramtha all alone, in the quiet of my room, or as I walk in the forest. He has been in my light since first I heard his name, for I knew him to be there, desired and deserved him to be with me.

I began to think of Ramtha as my own Spirit, and to open the doors for the unlimited perception to enter as knowingness. Consequently I expanded myself and my resources immediately and considerably. I have the audacity to desire *all things*, to want to *know* all things, yea to *BE* all things. This is the basis from which my impressions, my images and feelings come. I wrote this book not because I want you to believe what I believe, but because I *LOVE* what I AM! And it brings me untold JOY to share my feelings, which is all that Knowingness is.

I Love the grandeur of LIFE that is abundant and never ending. Each day is laden with excitement and a constant jubilation! All that surrounds is pregnant with the Thought from whence it springs and pulses. Each Thought brings ecstasy in my Being. Each moment is rich in learning and child-like exploration. It is difficult to stagnate when this is the attitude. And all that is necessary is a bit of perspective in your understanding. Ask your Spirit, the God of your Being, about a tree, a wave, relationships, the world, the universe. Ask your own God-head about anything that interests you, it will tell you anything you wish to receive. But you must be willing to listen, and it all comes in *FEELINGS*. You must be willing not to judge what you receive or compare and measure all things against something else.

Your Spirit is unlimited Thought, the first Thought.

The Science of Thought

All things have their basis, are derivative, of Thought. Thought is the ultimate creator of and sustaining Life Force behind all that IS. Were you able to remove the Thought from a single rose, the rose would be no more. The actual flower is the lowest vibration of the rose, and emanates continually the Thought that stands as its Creator, its Source. The Thought contains, as the highest vibration of the rose, its essence, the blueprint of the very rose and all of its parts. Its color, length of stem, number of leaves, texture of its petals and fragrant scent are all held in the Thought which surrounds and IS this single rose.

This is the case with all the myriad of forms and details of creativity existing on this beautiful planet. All Life stems directly from Thought, which is the highest vibratory influence that IS. Thought is the Life Force, the Primal Cause, the Directive Intelligence, the Source, the Mother-Father, Thought

IS GOD. I prefer the term God when referring to this Principle, and use it herein to mean pure Thought, pure reason. I hasten to point out that this Principle —God—has no ego personality, no judgment, for "He" is all that IS. To judge any one thing is to separate it from the perfect flow of Thought, which the Principle IS. This would never occur, for no thing is outside of the providence of God, all is derived from Thought-Principle.

Man is, under this reasoning, God. The flower is God. The sea, the mountain, the bird in its flight and the wind are all God. Man, however, is God in dominion over all of these, mineral, animal, and vegetable, for only Man has the power to receive, perceive, alter, judge, create from and *become* pure Thought. Man is able, through reason and emotion *combined*, to raise himself into the highest kingdom of all, which is unaltered God, pure reason, pure Thought. This is a simple process which anyone can accomplish, and no one is superior or inferior in the potential to receive pure Thought. ALL are Gods. That is the equanimity of the Father. All that is necessary is the desire and patience and reverence to allow this to occur— reverence for the body, and for the ego Self, for all people are complete and singular units of God-Thought-Principle. None is controlled from the outside. The Thought collectively seen in the attitude is the control, consequently to believe that you are being controlled is to have it so. This is your power and the power of each God.

Thought in its highest state, is devoid of color, sound and texture. It is elusive and free, and cannot be captivated. In the lowering of itself a mere fragment, it condenses and expresses itself as pure light that is white, with the Thought remaining ever present at the basis of this creativity. Outer space in its darkness and void is pure, unresolved Thought: God.

As the Thought condenses itself into light-synthesis, into color and sound (all light emits sound and sound is born of light—they are one in the same), it is seen and heard, as lower and lower it condenses and resolves into form, which is mass-synthesis, into matter, gross matter. This is the heaviest vibration of the Thought: mass. The creativity which allows this condensation to occur, is in an expansion of the Thought, for in its condensation it gathers unto itself energy, and thus becomes greater in its movement even into the next moment.

Life on this plane, which is the first plane of seven, is highly obsessed in what is termed the consciousness of matter and form: mass-consciousness. What we call "reality" and see and feel as texture on this plane is a result of mass-synthesis. What brought the mass into a fruition was the Thought. Your very body is a result of an ongoing Thought that the Father within you holds ever perfect and unaltered, into light, and into the expressed illusion of this vibration, which is mass. This mass is held together by Thought, which you are continually in receivership of. It is also possible to invert this creativity and take the body "up." In so doing one raises the body through feeling, in emotion and contemplative Thought, into a light principle, greater and quicker in its vibratory under-standing, and into pure Thought: God I Am.

This is the essence of Man, the essence of all Life: the *Thought* and its *realization* in pure *emotion*.

This process, this ascension of the flesh, is the natural order of things. It is God's design for us, *our* design for us, of Life.

The body was created not to exist a short moment, what we call a lifetime, and then to die. The body was created that Gods could experience this plane of creative form in a vehicle that vibrates at the same rate of activity as that form, until the desire is to be here no more in mass, and so return to a more expansive level of "consciousness," which is the Father-Principle.

The body was designed to live forever. Only the continual knowledge and expectancy of death and disease in cloistered thinking and limitation will kill it. One who realizes that he is God will bless the body, worship the body, and in contemplation of it and peace within the Beingness of it, and JOY in all of Life, raise the flesh into completion with God-Father.

Man who knows that he is God is termed *the Christ: God-Man, God realized in Man.*

Yeshua ben Joseph, or Jesus of Nazareth as he is known, is a Christ. Buddha before him knew full well that he was the Son of God-Principle, he merely called it by another name. Ramtha, Osiris, and a host of others whose names you do not know because they weren't on the most popular list, or because they weren't saviors or messiahs, all lived their lives on this plane in the conclusive demonstration that the Father dwells within them. They are all Christs. They live now and for eternity, for they ascended their bodies with them into the seventh understanding or plane, which is pure reason, pure God. This means that when they desire to return here they do not need to seek a ripe womb to give them a body and be here again as a babe and forget. They simply focus themselves wherever they desire to be, and in a Thought, they are here.

This is the age of Spirit, when all will become their own savior, this is the true messiah. I Am the Christ. I Am God in the highest order for I see myself to be this, and thus I AM.

ALL are the Christ, Gods manifesting perfectly their own reality and their own kingdoms. All men have the unique and singular perspective that lies within their own experience of Self. No other can have this exact perspective of them. It is through Self and the view of Self that lives are led and reality is formed, through each God's own vision of Self, his receptivity to Thought and openness to the emotion it generates. *Thought is no part of you until it is felt.*

The body is truly divine, it IS God. But it is only one part of the trinity, for each and every entity has also a Spirit and a Soul.

The Spirit is the God of your Being. It consists of the first spark, the first body of light below pure Thought that is and was, in the beginning of your beginnings, when the Father-Thought contemplated Himself and in so doing, expanded Himself.

These that came forth from the Universal Thought Principle are the Sons of God-Principle, the Christs, the perfect creations from the Mind of the Thought, into a singular movement. Each one is a complete and independent unit of God-Father. *All are this.* The Spirit is unlimited. It is the sieve onto the Ocean of Thought that IS the Source, the Father. It attracts to itself the thoughts which correspond to a feeling you are harboring or a thought you are pondering.

The Soul is the device which allows you to hold the image of the Thought that you might feel it, contemplate it, become it. Thought of itself is not recorded, held or stored. It is the pure, free, and elusive ongoingness that is the Father, that is the continuum called Life. The Soul is a recording device, a computer, as it were. It lies next to the heart, weighs thirteen ounces, and records all that occurs within the body and Spirit. All is recorded in emotion, in *feelings*. It is the Lord of your Being, for it is the compensation for your experience of the past seen collectively, and holds the feelings or collective image of you *for* you, in the NOW. The Soul of itself feels no emotion, but is a servant to the Spirit, to the ego totality, and maintains the bodily functions. (In the death of the body, it is the withdrawal of the Soul that takes the Life Force and departs with the Spirit). The emotion as it is felt in the Being, records itself in the Soul, moves outward into the auric structure, the light field around you, which is the Spirit. It becomes into light once again and is edified and crystallized in the aura as *feelings*.

This is called wisdom, and it comes from experiences. Knowingness is feelings. This light field which scientists have photographed and measured is the God of your Being, and it is pure *emotion*.

The brain does not store or record the Thought. It is a receiving unit into which Thought enters through the Spirit as light impulses. Here, it becomes electrical impulses and travels through the central nervous system the entire dimension of the body. It is perceived by the individual as feelings to reside finally in the Lord of the Being, the Soul, as emotions which equate to wisdom gained from experiencing the feeling.

Each Thought vibrates at its own specific frequency, and produces its own feelings which allows it to be identified. Only the Thoughts which you allow to enter will be felt and thus realized in your Being. On this plane of limited awareness only certain Thoughts are allowed to enter the brain-receiver. Those which are aligned with accepted thinking, mass-consciousness, or approved reality if you will, enter the brain in front through the upper right and left cerebrum and traverse the brain, sparked into comparable electricum to the lower base of the brain where they are collected by the fingers of the central nervous system at the base of the brain. This upper frontal portion of the brain-receiver is aligned with the alter-ego, which is the limited, judgmental, comparative thinking mind which filters Thoughts into right and wrong, acceptable or non-acceptable. The other Thoughts are simply deflected by this programmed ego-collective before they even enter the brain.

If a Thought is conceived in the mind of *one Man*, it is in the Mind of God, in the Ocean of Thought-Principle. If all Thought is God, why do we accept one Thought and reject another?

An unlimited Thought will be received only when the pituitary gland has been opened to activate a greater portion of the brain, which allows the Thought to be received. Scientists do not even know why the average individual uses approximately 11% of his brain capacity and no more. This average individual's brain is aligned with the spectrum of Thought which is form-conscious, mass-conscious. Until an entity conceives that there is more to be perceived, he remains closed to the infinity of knowledge which surrounds him.

When the pituitary opens, it activates a portion of the brain which is denser in its fluid (this is the conduit throughout the central nervous system also) and is aligned with an electricum at a greater speed, and higher vibratory understanding. This produces a feeling in the bodily structure which is of greater sensation and greater sensitivity—even on the surface of the skin—and a grandeur of emotion in the receptivity of this loftier capacity for feeling and awareness. With each more unlimited Thought, this gland opens more and more to activate more and more brain matter, to receive still a more unlimited Thought.

The pituitary is called the master gland, for it controls the functions and secretions of the other glands of the body. It is a ductless gland, the seventh of seven which are termed chakras or holy seals. They are doors to expression and can be enlarged at will, simply by placing the attention—the Thought—there, and desiring the greater flow of knowledge from the Ocean of Thought. Subtly and slowly, Thought by Thought they enlarge more and more, and as the pituitary opens like the petals of a lotus blossom, the channels open within your Being and allow greater awareness, greater knowingness in and of all things.

Thus, the Thought is received from the Ocean of consciousness, becomes sparked into light as it interacts with the Spirit which surrounds the body, into electricum in the brain-receiver, traverses the body as electrical impulses in the central nervous system, and is felt even to the tips of the fingers and toes. The electrical impulses register in the Soul as feelings, and continue on the journey back up the spinal column to the brain. The image of that Thought and its reception within the Being is transmitted through the sixth seal, which is located above the medulla oblongata and is called the pineal. From the pineal gland the image or sensation of the Thought is directed back into light-synthesis once again, and is transmitted into the auric structure—the Spirit—and into the Ocean of Thought.

This Thought draws to itself yet another that is like it in frequency and vibratory understanding. Like attracts unto like always, and so the Lord (Soul) and God (Spirit) of your Being are the inseparable totality of your infinite and eternal Being. They are in union and harmony as the creative flow of your ongoing Is-ness totality. The body is the vehicle which houses this flow, this phenomenon, in a tangible, three-dimensional form-reality. You draw to you ever that which will serve this growth, this flow in its ongoingness, which is Life. This is God to be sure.

*   *   *

Thought is remembered in the Soul as emotion. Memory is feeling. This feeling that you have about anything is called *Knowingness*. How do you know that your automobile is made of metal? Because you have touched it, seen it, driven in it, and all of this collectively in its structure you have been taught that it is called metal. Thus you KNOW that it is metal for you have a *feeling* about it. This is how you acquire knowledge about anything. Ponder this. Every Thought that IS generates its own feeling within you.

Thought surrounds everything as an Ocean of consciousness. Put your hand a few inches from your face and here is the Ocean in its flow, here is the Father-God. To know *anything* merely say, "From the Lord God of my precious Being, I now *know* that I *KNOW*." Then allow yourself to *feel* the knowingness. Too simple? God, in an uninhibited flow is the purest simplicity there IS, for that is how pure knowingness occurs.

The complexities and perplexities are a result of limited perception. Your vision of you is the Treasurer of your Kingdom. Think about it. Only Man can separate himself or any other thing from the perfect flow of Thought. The Source would never do this. When Man judges anything, he actually separates himself from it and thus minimizes and judges himself. To say "I KNOW" and be willing to stand behind that and *feel* it, signals the Soul into awareness and allows the emotion to be recognized and the Thought to be received, to come forth. This receivership signals the brain into greater activity and the answer, the Thought, enters into the consciousness as feelings. This is called "psychic" ability, it is really simply *God* ability and ALL are equally capable. All that is required is patience and practice *knowing*.

The brain (body), Soul and Spirit were designed to house a complete and knowing God. To ascend is to return with the body into light, into Thought-Principle, but you can know everything NOW if you desire. Simply open the Soul and allow unlimited feeling. Open the mind, which opens the brain and allows unlimited Thought to enter in. To accomplish this it is necessary to learn not to judge or alter the Thought or the feeling. To master the seventh, to become unlimited, is not to master your Thoughts or control them. You cannot, for they are pure and elusive God essence. To master the seventh is to master the judgment against them, to *feel* them and discover from whence they came. They ARE for a reason you know. Ponder all that you feel and all that you are. It is all God.

*   *   *

Thought is a subtle essence to Man on this plane, for he is accustomed to the heaviness of mass in its sensations. It requires patience, and most of all Love of Self in order to learn to perceive Thought in its unaltered purity. In order to accomplish this it is also necessary to reckon the ego understanding of Self.

Ego

In all that we are, we see ourselves as individual and unique, and we truly are. Pure ego is pure God. It is the singular movement in all that IS, that is the Father *completely* in and of itself. The Father is the plural ongoingness and the Son, the Christ, is the singular expression of this plural.

Ego was born when the Spirit took to itself a child—the Soul—that it could hold the Thought in an image to contemplate it, and thus have an individual and unique perspective upon that Thought. It is to each and every ego aspect of the Divine Whole —which is you—that the Father gives the free will that is Love in its purest essence. Ego is your individual identity within the Source, and exercising the choices that make your Life different from all others.

Then what is the alter-ego? Altered ego is altered God. That is to say, that when the pure Oneness and Is-ness that is our natural relationship with the Source of Life, is altered by one man's perception to cause him to feel lessened or threatened by his own illusion of limitation, that Christ, that God-Man is acting out altered God. Thus he is not reflecting the entirety of the Father within himself, but only expresses a limited aspect. Thus he suffers and bemoans his fate to be so forlorn and unimportant in the cosmos and in his meager life. He sees his fragile ego only in comparison to others, and it takes control of his perception of *all* things to insure that this limited scope is adhered to always, and so it becomes the standard by which all Life is measured. And so anything that does not fit into this scope of consciousness is rejected as unreal, illusion or impossible. It is the plane of three-dimensional mass-synthesis that powerfully weaves him into its web, and asks that all things be measured by *its* nature, which is only one aspect of the Father-Source.

And when he labors to master the elements, or to make a bit of gold or silver that his family might eat well and enjoy warmth and comfort, he forgets that the real treasure of these moments is not the accomplishment of the task or the structure which he has built, but the satisfaction that derives from participation on this level of creativity, which is a *feeling*.

When many are gathered together to share a grand holiday meal and the preparation of succulents, good wine and tender meats, the one who insists that he knows best and even becomes less than happy if things are not exactly as they should be, may be correct. But he has robbed himself of a greater joy, and the union and delight of sharing creatively with other Gods, as he concerns himself—and so defines himself—by the results in mass, and not the feelings, which are the real prize of the experience. He will even go against his brother's feelings without sensitivity to them in order that the comparatively unimportant task is performed as he deems "correct." Are not the feelings of another more dear than a mere meal out of so many? All must reason this for themselves to ascertain their own priorities; but all have witnessed this kind of situation and felt the vibration in their Being. When the gathering has dispersed and the food is forgotten, often the small indifferences of one to another still linger in the Soul as a sorrow or misunderstanding which separates men and causes pain, and this becomes the predominating feeling of the occasion as a memory which is very powerful.

When you pass this plane into the greater planes of God, no gold nor possessions of any sort are taken. What is forever in your Being that is the bounty of your expression here or anywhere, is the *emotions*. Emotions are all that we are. The limited ego will embroil you into a squirrel-cage like circle of a thought that generates an automatic reaction emotion, that draws a similar thought, generating a similar emotion that you cherish not, time after time, until you dismantle the squirrel-cage by taking a moment to realize your own sovereignty. You are not a mass-concept-thinking-machine. You are a God, the Sovereign-Being-Ruler of your own perspective understanding. Undertake to understand these feelings by putting them into a grander view.

This is your divine power of reason. *KNOW* that you are One with the Father, never losing your singular individuality, but *holding to no ideal save your own*.

This brings the altered ego to its knees, for the altered ego insists that you follow the fashion of the mass, or the prescribed rituals of a saint or guru. Become your own ideal of you for you, and you are God Sublime. Follow no one, for who can see you as you do or Love you as greatly? Only you can be God for you, for eternity this has been the case if you'll look around to see it. Who has ever died for you? Who has ever lived for you? Only you.

Become the pure Ego aspect of the Father-Principle that you feel—embrace Self. This is the Is-ness that is ongoing, that is Life Eternal. This is the Godfire within you.

THE FOLLOWING PAGE IS BLANK.
IT IS FOR YOU TO WRITE A POEM OR A STORY
ABOUT *YOURSELF*.

EXPRESS YOUR FEELINGS, YOUR *LOVE* FOR
YOU.

REALLY GET INTO IT. DESCRIBE YOUR TALENTS,
YOUR BEAUTY, YOUR UNIQUE ABILITIES AND
PERFECT UNDERSTANDING OF *YOU*.

DO NOT DENY YOURSELF THIS OPPORTUNITY
BY BEING MODEST. *SAVOR* YOURSELF FOR A
MOMENT OR TWO.
GO AHEAD!

DO NOT SHOW THIS TO ANYONE.

A Moment

Behold, God is a moment.

How beautiful is the NOW. Languorous, crystal clear, sensing all that you are, *feel* the moment.

Watch the tree shimmer as it calls to the luscious breeze.

Hear the daffodils sing their tunes of delight? They know only *Life*.

They know only *NOW*.

Feel the water lap the shore, and so it titillates your sensors, expanse of color, untiring light reflections for your Eye only. Smell the spray, the luster of the element, the secrets hidden within. As you watch and listen to NOW, you'll begin to realize that the element of dimension is your directive. Time and space are illusions that are relative to *you*, not the other way 'round.

Feel the texture of all that you can see in every direction. Hear the joy of all sound that surrounds you, whatever it is.

Experience the NOW inside you, and KNOW that this is all that *IS*. There is no thing greater in Life than this moment. You have the power to make it anything you wish. If you're bored or malcontent, change something! Yours is the free will to explore any avenue, or no avenue at all. Use this moment to *become* you, to find joy in YOU.

Now is the greatest you've ever been. All you've been has led you to this point of Beingness, this moment, and the collective expression of you is *this moment* and how you *see* it. That is the awesome power you possess. Only with patience will you experience the NOW (or any other time) more fully. Patience allows PEACE to transfix itself in your Being. It allows the limits and expectations to fall away, and you begin to realize that those things are not really your boundaries.

You're far greater than a definition in time or space—which is time measured laterally. You are the *creator* of the illusions, whether they surround and protect, or limit and define you. They give you an image and definition to society and friends, but more importantly they give you an image of you for yourself. So they clarify your position for others in an interaction, but what of when you are all alone?

FEEL the moment. If your moments aren't joyful, know that they can be. Know that you are in control of them. *Whatever you accept, you become.* If the illusions that surround you aren't pleasing, you must ask yourself—why? All that causes you to feel less, or compares you to another, or brings you displeasure in the Thought of it, drop it all away for but a *MOMENT*. Give yourself this gift: one moment, for however long you judge this to be, of contemplative Thought concerning *NOW*.

Listen, watch, smell, feel the enormity of the present. It is simple to pretend to be at peace. Imagining it, pretending it, allows the Soul to feel it whether you believe it or not. Pretend you ARE it, pretend you always have been. Fantasize the NOW into any delightful thing you choose, and lo and behold you're FEELING it. Then, slowly and surely the Soul becomes accustomed to this feeling and begins to remind you of it in the body, in your attitude, and in your Life. Peace is a simple state of allowing yourself to BE.

If you've ever had a fear, you've done this very thing with your imagination and you've felt it deeply, and sometimes the fear has come to pass.

Why not try it with something wonderful and know that by doing so you are opening the channels for it to come forth in the same manner? All give so much credence to the past and their guilt, or the future and their fears and apprehensions. To be God is to give power in your Thoughts and emotions to the present, to the all-consuming NOW. Give yourself a present of the present.

Navigate your moments as the Lord of a great ship. Take them wherever your desires lead you. Your desires are your creative fuel. Spontaneity can teach you so much, but you must let go of expectations of what "should be" in order to truly feel the moments. Cherish them. Become them.

Ramtha says, a moment is "the exhilaration at the height or depth of a Thought."

As I began to listen to my body, I perceived that to raise this mass, this heavy form back into a light-principle, I needed to get the energy flowing faster and freer. The Easterns call this energy which flows up through the body, "shakti." This shakti can be made to move quicker and with more intensity simply by placing the Thought at the root or first seal, and drawing it up through the center of the body to the crown (pituitary) or seventh seal. As this occurs it lifts the body in its rate of vibration, and stimulates the pituitary which controls the input level of the brain itself.

The first seal is located in the genitals. It is the root energy, the greatest energy in the body. Used in this way the sexual energy in my Being was transformed into contemplative Thought, and I became aware of my Spirit as it lifted my body to heights I'd never dreamed of.

When the body is lifted and tendered, Loved and respected, it opens the brain-receiver, the Soul, and the entirety of the Being that all can be seen, felt, known. This begins simply by feeling "hot" in the loins or womb, as the case may be, and driving this heat or energy upward through the crown of the head.

As the sixth seal (pineal) enlarges it amplifies the images that you wish to draw into your kingdom as they are fed into the Ocean of Thought, and into your aura where they act as an electro-magnet. Then you begin to draw these things to you as you learn to manifest and *become in feelings* that which you design and desire.

*   *   *

*   *   *

I lie in bed upon waking
Contemplation of this form, bodily movement
Peculiar structure
Beautiful.

I ponder, I expand
Toes, calves, thighs
Heartbeat swells to a surge of heat
Glowing in my temples even as the palms quiver.
Eyes roll upward inward
Forehead pulses
Sucks toward me all signals, all Light
Wondrous seventh pituitary seal
Channels open.

Body leaps and lurches
As though I'll climb out of my skin!
Sweet sweat
Flesh tingles, crawls, moves.

45

Great New Day I Greet You!
Perfect Son of the Perfect Cause
Christ I Am!
GOD I AM!

I align myself with the Spirit-God in all things
Body is lifted
Body is lighter.
Spirit Body
Unlimited Covenant of my Father-God
Contemplate *this*. . . .

From deep within the cavern of my Being
Quicken the flesh
Vibration of each cell
Soul of each cell (each one has a nucleus of pure
    light you know)
Faster lighter glowing
The Breath within the Breath
Resonating New Life
EXHILARATION!

New Day.
Now.
Moment IS.
Divine Celebration.
I Am the embodiment of it.

Life.

Ramtha contemplated the wind some thirty-five thousand years ago upon a hilltop, a bluff more exactly, and watched it sweep down through his encampment and blow everything about. He watched it turn the leaves of the olive tree from a deep green to a sudden flicker of silvery slips of light. He gazed as it took up a maiden's skirts while she waded in a stream, and bared her sweet calves and knees to his hidden eyes.

The wind had force, but was invisible: enigma. It caressed and sang yet was, of a sudden, calm: elusive. Ramtha conceived the wind to have unlimited freedom. It enticed him to imagine how the wind would fly, where it went, what it saw, and so he began to visualize himself *as* the wind.

He imagined how everything would look sailing in the magic free wind, until one day he found himself high over the land looking down upon a speck that was his body. It startled him and even frightened him, and immediately he found himself again in his own flesh.

It was only after many years of intense desire to repeat this feat and finally giving up, that he had another out-of-body experience. He discovered that it was relaxation of the body and a sense of peace within himself that eventually allowed him to learn to leave the body at will.

Then, after years of contemplation and numerous forays out of his body through the Spirit of his Being, Ramtha began to have his body guarded that he might leave it for longer periods in order to learn to take it with him. This he conceived of all alone in the quiet of his Thoughts, though none other had ever done it or even understood what he was talking about.

Thus, he eventually succeeded, ascending body and all into the wind and into what is called the Seventh Heaven. Sixty-two times he ascended before his final demonstration to all his peoples. This he performed on the north-east bank of the Indus River, witnessed by many who had been led there by him, all beloved by him, and whom he promised he would return one day.

And so, Ramtha has returned, though he never really left, and through this magnificent channel named J. Z. Burnett he teaches thousands, and lifts his brethren all across this country through his unlimited perspective and knowingness.

J. Z. teaches also. She is far more than "just a channel." Her own knowingness is profound, and she has a genius for expressing that knowingness in the simplest of terms, that all can understand and become. With or without Ramtha she is a great God, a sublime and dedicated Light in the Heavens of so many. I Love her dearly and eternally, and continually learn much from my talks and meetings with her.

Just as J. Z. is not dependent on the Ram for her knowledge—she takes it directly from the Source, her own Spirit—so Ramtha is not dependent on J.Z. in his communication with this plane, though she is his only full channel. As I have stated, my greatest communion with Ramtha has been as an unseen presence, without a word, alone with the elements and in openness to my own Spirit which is as infinite and knowing as Ramtha's. I emphasize this because it is important for Man to understand that he is all-knowing, right where he stands. There are no pre-requisites and no external guide is needed if you open to the God of *your* Being. This is Ramtha's first teaching and J. Z.'s greatest example to us. It is the wellspring from whence this book arises. It is a truth which I have *become* and which I live, and the constant demonstration of this has made me an eternal sovereign unto myself.

Ramtha's story about the wind and his ascension made me yearn for an image that would be as powerful for me. I tried the contemplation of the wind, but it just wasn't *my* image. I listened to Ramtha speak of his only teachers being the elements, the sun and moon, the trees and early dawn sky as the light filters through, and the seasons and their steadfastness. One day, though I wasn't at all cold, I was struck with the idea of building a fire. I watched the paper catch first and ignite the smaller twigs and kindling, and at last the flames that licked the great cedar log I'd placed on top became a blaze of golden-red light. I sat and pondered just how it is that fire IS.

The paper is composed mostly of carbon. The molecules are set to moving faster as the match is applied to the material. The flame is the result of the oxygen of the air fueling the heightened motion of the carbon-oxygen marriage.

This is a simplified explanation of the burning process, but this is the information that I received as I sat and asked the Source about the nature of fire. And further imagery was added. The wood is a symbol of the body, or mass-synthesis. The match is the Thought being applied to the mass with the desire to transmute the mass into a different form. The flame represents the Spirit and exemplifies the Thought in its light vibration or light body drawing the mass into expansion and into light-synthesis. This intensifies the flame until the entire mass is eventually transmuted into light-synthesis, into the desired form(lessness) through the continual application of Thought-synthesis, into Universal Substance.

I sat for days, heaping log upon larger log onto the blaze, and losing myself in the flames and embers. When I closed my eyes all I could see was a flame (any wonder?) and I began to visualize my own Spirit Body surrounding me as a flame, ever brighter, lighter and more expansive. It permeates each molecule, each nerve tissue, each bone, the marrow, the muscle; each cell of my Being I could see and *feel* heightened, quickened, moving faster and freer. The consciousness of each cell in its central spark basis becomes lighter as every part of the body is aflame with the Spirit!

It sent me reeling with spasms of ecstasy and from this point all I needed to do was contemplate my Spirit, and my body responded with a raised vibration, a "high" that is beyond any I've ever known. With each new moment it only intensifies in its tone and frequency. The body will shake and sweat at first, but it rallies to the Cause and the Soul weeps at the expression of itself, for there are no words to equate what this feeling brings to the Being in memory and ecstatic joy. The memory is of Oneness with the Father, and this is what is returning my body into a pure Light-Principle from whence it came.

The image of fire reminds me of a phenomenon which is called "spontaneous human combustion." It is an occurrence in the Being, in the Thought and its perfect clarity of reception which, when allowed to enter and ring forth in the body, raises it in a brilliant moment into a blaze of light and into the realm of pure Thought. This is the seventh plane of understanding and, in short, spontaneous human combustion is ascension.

Entities who've come to their own singular awareness of the Oneness in which they see themselves with all things, and who have pondered and perfected themselves to a state of blissful non-judgment and LOVE of *all* that they see and are, in one grand instant they find that the body is a wisp of light, as the body is raised into unlimited Spirit essence.

The overstuffed chair on which they sat will be found with a little pile of debris, or ashes as they call it. But the chair and all that surrounds it will be unmarred and unaffected. It is an energy which is more brilliant than a hundred suns which takes the body back into light, yet it is gentle and peaceful, for the entity has prepared for it and accepted the translation of Self into a volatile emotion.

This phenomenon has been documented, but few on this plane know exactly what occurs or why. I assure you that the entity who ascends into Thought, without formerly knowing that it is even possible, while perhaps startled, soon realizes the whys and wherefores. It is a simple and natural thing to ascend. While this combustion method is not my choice, it is ascension none-the-less and worthy of mention.

*   *   *

As my light field grows stronger, the light core of each cell is drawn into greater alignment with Spirit, allowing a greater flow of electric current through the central nervous system. As the Thought/light/electricum becomes more intense, water is sometimes retained within the cells in order to facilitate this re-alignment. Water is the conduit through which the nerve impulses travel and occasionally the legs, arms, and hands swell up with this retention.

Each cell of the body is aligned perfectly with the collective attitude within the Being. As the attitudes change and consciousness broadens, the cells adjust accordingly to accommodate each new heightened vibration. This also entails throwing off what are called toxins, which are really simply elements that the body no longer needs. At times my bowels run and my limbs ache, and the temperature of the body rises considerably in a fever of this detoxification. The head burns and aches as the upper seals expand within the cranium. This has occurred many times, often painful, but on each successive occasion it is diminished. Each episode, though uncomfortable, is a blessing. I can promise you that the uplifting and reckoning of the body is worth any and all of the comparatively minor discomfort.

Ramtha likens the body to an internal combustion machine. The cells hold a spark and the blueprint of their design in the RNA-DNA structure. The circulatory system supplies the fuel both as nutrients, which the cell can use only in the gaseous state, and as oxygen carried from the lungs. As the Thought/electricum travels through the central nervous system, it ignites the oxygen, explodes within the spark of each cell, and propels the cell into reproducing itself. The Thought is ever being applied to the cells, for without it the reproduction ceases and Life does not continue within the body. As the nutrients are absorbed in combination with the oxygen, an oxide results as a by-product which the body must release. The pituitary produces enzyme-hormones which accomplish the task of balancing the body in its nutrients and wastes. One enzyme in particular, an oxide removing agent called S.O.D. (superoxide dismutase) is produced in the pituitary and transferred across a bridge to the pineal where it is distributed into the bloodstream. This enzyme is secreted in generous amounts until an entity reaches puberty, at which time its production ceases. Then the cells begin to age, and slowly the body is allowed to die. Without this enzyme the cells retain these oxide wastes, and reproduction of cells is inhibited and eventually ceases. S.O.D. can be purchased in most vitamin shops and drug stores, and when taken in quantities of four to six per day it allows the body tissues to rejuvenate themselves inside and out. Thus aging is retarded, and can actually be reversed.

Another new formula is now available, it is called Gerovital H3 (GH3). It was developed by Dr. Ana Aslan in Roumania, and is a delicate balance of elements which promotes an enzyme-hormone (Harmony) balance within the pituitary and pineal glands, thus promoting a feeling of peace and harmony in the central nervous system, and has been extensively proven to restore youth to the body both in appearance and in feeling. This, along with S.O.D. is a wondrous benefit to the body, and I urge everyone I know to take them both!

Most important of all is a Loving attitude toward Self, and the acceptance and Love of the body itself. The enzyme-hormones can be greatly assisted with a balance of *minerals* as well as vitamins—including vitamin F—which all together will promote the rejuvenation of the skin, the inner organs, and peace of mind, and thus certainly aid the actual ascension of the body itself.

*   *   *

An important factor in consciously raising the physical vibrations is to remain relaxed. Any tension or holding in the body, while not harmful certainly, will only inhibit the flow and full sweep of energy. This active and conscious drawing up of the shakti through the body is very powerful, and directs the attention inward, to the spark within. I found it especially lifting and helpful while living in New York, surrounded by a heavy consciousness fabric, one that insists that you serve its expectations, rather than serving you who are the creator of it. Thus, the God within me became my joy, my inner strength and fulfillment. Raising the bodily movement into a grander expression of the God I Am is a power that I took boldly and happily.

All I could think of was ascending, and I spent hours just sitting in my chair contemplating my body and consciously raising the shakti through my Being, until I was exhausted and exhilarated at once. This practice took me into a new and wonderful awareness of my body and an understanding that I'd lacked for so long. It aligned my Thoughts with the divine Life Force that is *within*. It affected my body profoundly, but more importantly it affected my *attitude* about my body.

In moments of fire or Self-judgment I was reminded of the God I Am. But when the fire subsided and I left the city for the forest by the sea, I could readily perceive this great truth: All that is really necessary to ascend the body is Self Love, peace and *JOY*. For when an entity Loves Self, he Loves all that surrounds him and joy is immanent.

Joy is the highest state that Man can attain, and experienced and allowed to bubble forth from within the Being, it raises the vibratory understanding and allows Love to be perceived in *all things*. This is all it takes to raise the flesh into an ascended principle. The methods, even the ones I have related from my own experiences, are not necessary. In fact they even get in the way of the full sweetness of JOY of the moment. Love is all that is necessary for Love *IS* the Father. When you Love you, you will not remain limited by this plane and its narrowness of accepted Life, and you will never die. This plane and its collective illusions and games cannot hold one who Loves freely.

But most find this simple act of Loving Self to be the most difficult thing of all. Allow me to share my simple understanding of this aspect of God, this feeling called Love.

Love

In the beginning was the Thought, motionless movement, of itself pure and unto itself all consuming.

As the Thought contemplated itself and expanded into the great Lights that came forth, the Sons of the Great Thought, the power that allows this expansion into ongoingness to BE, is LOVE.

The Sons went forth into the farthest perimeters of Thought and eternity, and when the Father looked into His wondrous Sons, He saw Himself and was most pleased. The beautiful and radiant Son is a perfect reflection of His most sublime and perfect Self.

And when the Sons looked back into the Father-Principle-Cause, they saw themselves reflected perfectly *as* the Father. Thus did the Father bestow His greatest gift upon His most glorious creation, the original Covenant with Him, Benevolent Father: *FREE WILL.*

The Sons of God went forth into the expanse of Thought that is the Father, and created universes of light, mass, planes of expression aligned with individual attitudes, and worlds of emotion and experiences all grand, and all created from the substance that IS the Father, but all created *by* the Son.

The Love of the Father that allows the Son to express *anything*, and gives him free will even to limit himself to a plane of limitation and illusion and worship it as inescapable "reality" (even to a lacking,) this Love and perfect free will that is never judged by the Father has been forgotten to a great extent here.

To Love another freely, to expect *nothing* from him save that he BE, is to Love as the Father Loves. Indeed it is to *become* the Father.

All wish to be Loved, for they remember the perfect Love that is held for them in the Mind of the Father. All wish to Love, which is to express this grand recognition of Self. And so, Man scurries about in life after life on this plane, embroiled in emotions, needs and desires, dreams most unfulfilled, enslaving others and so being enslaved, sacrificing and sometimes finding happiness, but all of this in quest for Love. . . .

To understand Love more clearly all must reason this within themselves: *The essence of Love is FREE WILL.* The only thing ever created that is the Father completely in a singular movement, thus able to *become* as the Father in all that He IS, is Man (Son). Thus, the Lifestream for Man from God is Love. Of all that Gods (Sons) have created, as the Ram says, "Love is the glue that holds it all together."

As the Father gave the covenant to the Son, so it is given continually and renewed each moment. So it IS and so it shall BE for all eternity. No thing shall ever be created that can take from you the Life Force, for you are the Father singly and totally within your Being, and equal to all others. The Father would never create anything to limit or destroy you, for to what purpose when you are an *expression of Him*?

Thus you have dominion over you and all that you bring into manifested creativity from your own unique stance on the banks of the Ocean of Thought. Thus, to participate even in a world of total illusion (which is reality) is to be One with the

Father, though you believe (thus know) that you are not. You *are* the free will that is Love from God-Principle.

On this plane, the first plane and the plane of solid mass and form synthesis, Gods once existed in harmony, one with the other and with all things, in a peaceful coexistence and in knowingness of the Godhead. In this realized Oneness, Gods created bodies to explore this plane of understanding and their created forms. They wanted to experience their creations directly, and these vehicles were experiments designed to suit the concepts of these Gods who had never before been in weighty flesh.

Man lived in peace and equality until one God determined that he was closer to the Source than all others. He even determined that the Source was a singular entity, one with greater powers, for he had forgotten the utter freedom that he had possessed before his descent into mass. He named himself "Priest" and gave himself authority on the Will of the Divine Principle. Those who would not agree or comply with his concept and dictum regarding the Father, were cursed as being separate from God. Those who feared the unknown feared this singular God and believed in Priest, giving up their free choice of expression and responsibility over Self.

In allowing fear to rule them, the threats of Priest became very powerful. As more followed, the Thought of a collective multitude augmented his power and soon his predictions came to pass. When there are so many expecting an event, it is given credence to occur. Soon there were many priests, and as superstition grew their power grew proportionally. Those who would not follow were a threat to the priests, and so were cast away from the group as "damned." Thus the curse "God damn you" was born. It generates even to this day a remembrance of utter loss and despair. To be separated from the Father, to be lowered and left in a place of weakness where one can never raise oneself back into "grace" so-called, this was the greatest horror for Man in early times on this plane.

Thus priests gained control of the peoples and enslaved the lot of them into thinking and acting out their dogmatic will rather than Self will. And so duality was born. Good (God) and evil (devil) became polarized concepts of the unknown, and God the Father-Principle, egoless Source, became God the judge, vengeful and fearsome, a thing outside of Man. With this came the ultimate separation: death.

Until this time Man lived without a Thought or concept of death. The Father, which was the Source of all movement and eternity, was only

LIFE. Death came only with the absolute certainty that without the approval and recognition of the herd—the established churches and society that was ruled by them—one is surely lost, lowly, and pitifully alone: separate.

This superstition prevails even today that the Father is a personality, an ego to whom we owe idolatry and emulation, and one who could cast us off as soon as welcome us into his "fold." Thus, the Love that was once all that the God of our Being— our Spirit—was, is replaced in the mind of Man as being dual, fearful, right vs. wrong: judgmental.

And so, in the Soul of Each Man involved, the Father takes an unsure position. Each Man, each God allows this to occur in his Being. Each God chooses his attitude, his experience, and no one is on this plane because he is less advanced or less worthy. There is no "working things out" that forces anyone to be here. We are all here because we *want* to be, we have chosen it. There is no working out required, *save that you choose to*. There is only experiences. All who come to this plane or any other, do so by choice, and are free to leave and travel among the planes and dimensions at any time. But this is accomplished only with Love.

The virtue that accompanies Love, and Loving in freedom, is forgiveness. To forgive anyone for anything is to forgive Self. For how is it that forgiveness is needed except that you have seen it that way and so harbored these feelings in yourself? When all is seen in its moment as purposeful good, and coming from free will, then all is evenly seen as the Father and there is no thing that requires forgiveness. No one is a victim without allowing it to be so. And to forgive yourself for *everything* is merely to observe that you have previously seen things with a limited perspective.

To advance in your Godhead and in your vision it is necessary to learn to Love in freedom. This begins by Loving *YOU*. To Love unequivocably is to become aware that all that is in your Life, all people, conditions, labors, seasons, attitudes and actions are indeed and quite simply the Beloved Father, which is *YOU*.

When you look into the eyes of your woman, your husband, your enemy or a stranger, you will begin to see readily your own reflection, your own essence in the eyes of that God. And when you ponder the great tree and the flower, the sun and oceans of this glorious planet, you will readily perceive the Father in them, for it is *you* who created these in the Father's stead.

Why do all wish to Love and be Loved? We are in remembrance of the Father, of supreme Love which is unlimiting, vast and wild, a free moving essence which allows *everything* simply to *BE*. To begin to recapture this feeling, one must begin with the Source of Love, and it comes from within. No one can teach it to you. No one can ever Love you as you do or give to you from the outside what you have not conceived of within. You must delve inward and give it to Self first. Then you are perfectly aligned with the Father within you, for that is all that He desires for you. Then you are Loving you as He does. It is most freeing, I can assure you.

And if you go within and find fear, this comes from the unknown. Replace it with the *conclusive knowingness* that no thing exists in the providence of God Supreme that can harm you or take from you anything that truly belongs to you. And if you find yourself alone, bless it and bless yourself and Love it, for your greatest moments will be spent in *wordless wonder* of *you*.

There is a purposeful good (God) in all estates, and an understanding of this in a practical application in your Life will bring you complete freedom from measure, and your Life will begin to flow. Your rewards will be manifold and your peace will issue forth from deep within that nothing can pierce it. Be at peace in Loving you. Be *joyful* in your moments. This will take you into eternity and into the seventh, for it is the highest state of God. Simply Love all things and allow yourself to BE. Contemplate these things and allow them to enter your consciousness as *feelings*. The intellect will understand them for they are the utmost in simplicity. It may also fight them for it has been trained to compare and judge and measure all things, where these things are immeasureable.

The intellect has nothing to do with Love, and proof is never important where Love is present. In these feelings, however, you will recognize the truth for yourself. Do not accept my truth, become your own feelings. This is your truth and it is here that you will become God. It is within that all will manifest for you, and it will occur as feelings.

Receivership

... seated on the shore I feel the blue, soaking it in through my skin ... two levels, one the water, one the sky, a mountain in between.... clouds lilt by in the lofty winds, puffing, rolling, undulating, sweeping, all layers, all forms ... blue into indigo into violet, crimson rimmed with gold ... light sprays through blowing curtains from the ceiling of the sky. ...

*   *   *

Each cloud feels different, try it! Put yourself into a cloud, really become it, feel what it is to BE a cloud. It tingles on the skin, behind the ears, the pulse between the eyes receives the knowingness: where it's going, where it's been, what it's made of. You ARE it.

I see the breeze whisper in the cedar boughs, feel it crackle in my aura and suck itself through

71

the head, and whooosh into the spine as my heart *leaps* as it enters the Soul with emotion, with glee! I feel the vibration of the Thought itself.

Now it's overcast. Rains drench the entire universe, slam onto the roof. The sound is melodious monotony. The color outside is barely color—hazy gray, slate chalk murky. It has a texture of forever —cool, soft, aqueous substance, universal substance. When I contemplate the rains over the fertile land I feel them through my entire body. My Being feels like it goes into forever. And it does, for I Am at peace within my Being, and that is the feeling of forever.

Feeling is what it's all about. The Thoughts surround you as an Ocean, but what gives the Thought credence in the Being is the feeling it generates. The Thought is no part of your Being until it is felt.

I knew this in my intellect, and had felt it deeply enough to rearrange my whole Life, leave the city and move to a cabin on the water, and establish my first priority as "Being." But it was not until I opened myself in the deepest way that I truly felt the clarity of a Thought as it is received and felt, with all the doors open, no judgment and no "understanding," which, in our complex lives is completely comparative. It is a way of receiving that

I can only describe as the stripping off of all the masks that define and measure, and they come off gradually in layer upon layer. As the masks come off, there becomes less and less need to "understand" anything, for you simply *become* that thing which you're experiencing. To receive a Thought and feel it to the depth of the fiber of the Being and explore it in your own individual context, this is unlimited God.

One evening as I walked the beach I contemplated ecstasy. I felt the wind on my face and tasted the lusty air and the twilit sky. As I stood on the shore, the surf washed in and out so softly, so evenly. I crouched down on my haunches with the water rolling right over my shoes. I wanted to be right *in* the water, to have it envelope me up to my shoulders. I wanted to BE the water.

As I felt the water within my Being, a phrase I'd uttered countless times came through my consciousness, though I did not "think" of it, or hear it or say it. I simply felt and *became* it: "The Father and I are One." At that moment I looked up to the edge of water rippling down the beach. I saw the horizon and its soft light meet the water. I was aware of my own outline and form only as it melted into all of these. My body seemed to disappear, and in that instant I became profoundly aware of the total absence of boundaries separating me from water or sky or mountain or cloud. I felt what it is to *become* the things which I observed.

My Spirit expanded, took on the feeling of the Spirit of all things. The essence of the very earth I walk became clear to me, for it is inside of me. The Father is within me, for only as I *feel* the expression of God in any one thing is it perceived by me. Only then do I know it. Only as I see and feel a person or a tree within my Soul are they a part of my experience, and a part of me.

Now, I must tell you that I'd known this in my head as theory for quite a while. It was only when I felt it demonstrated conclusively in my *experience* and with physical sensations, that I *became* this knowingness.

This is knowingness realized, when you *become* the feeling, and so *become* the person or the tree or the Thought. To be in receivership of these feelings, these Thoughts, this is the trick. Some are uncomfortable, some are downright painful when viewed alone, that is, without the perspective of divintiy that is the eternal basis of your Beingness. But to arrive at a place where you can accept *all* feelings without judging them or separating yourself from them, this is ultimate freedom. Then you are a great and sovereign God, capable of expressing anything, and able to relate to all life in a *Oneness* with it.

*   *   *

I watch the water lap the shore, waves roll steadily
Inward
Constant
Tireless, knowing only NOW.

O Teach me Sea
   Teach me to be steadfast, peaceful, constant
   To be buoyant in all moments, JOYFUL!
   Teach me evenness, to ride the waves of my
      emotion
   To reflect the Light, exquisitely and with my own
   Character.

O Remind me of the vast expanse of my Being
   The Ocean of the
   Depth within
   Teach my voice to (whspr) softly gently such as
      the sand
   Receives the flow
   So I become the Flow, serenity, resolve.

O Teach me to be still, content
   To be as the Sea,
   To merely
   BE.

*   *   *

To have a feeling that you'd label "bad" is to experience an emotion that does not fit in with your programming of what "should be." But each time you push these feelings down or back or away from your conscious reckoning, you're closing a door in your Being, in the mind and in your Soul. Every time you reject a Thought or feeling, you judge it, negate it and separate it from yourself. Now even a "bad" Thought or uncomfortable emotion is the Father, for all things are. When you reject anything or limit yourself to or away from anything, you are limiting your own expression of the Father. You are willing to be one part of the Father, but not all of Him.

If you spend just a moment with this feeling that is so unacceptable and ponder WHY you have it, what caused it and how to reckon it in an understanding within you, you'll conquer it in yourself. To conquer something is not to be rid of it, but to take the darkness away and see it calmly and evenly. To contemplate anything peacefully and slowly takes a bit of the fire and confusion away. Then you begin to see that you are in control of the experience and the emotion, not the other way around. Then, the next time this same Thought comes to you, it will generate a different feeling. You can choose to have it, to explore it, or to move into the next moment with joy in your capacity to feel and understand. Then you aren't cloistering yourself to an allotted group of emotions that limit you to a herd-consciousness that is the approved reality.

When you contemplate a feeling or a Thought, you expand the alter-ego in its sheath, to encompass and become this new part of you. This is how the altered ego becomes, slowly but surely, expansive in its (your) understanding to encompass and become *unaltered God*. This is a God expressing in an unlimited flow of Thought, and emotion realized from Thought.

Merely speak to your Soul and communicate that this feeling is now seen as the Father, and does not minimize or negate your own Love of Self. Command the alter-ego to be at peace and to accept this new Thought. When you discover more information regarding this feeling or situation, in a greater understanding and compassion for Self and peace within your Being, you will open doors for more peace, more understanding, which brings more compassion for Self and for everything else.

I can tell you that when you are aware of the re-programming that you have achieved in your Soul, the next time that "bad" Thought arrives it will bring you great joy in your Being, for you will find that it no longer defines you, but rather embellishes Self. Your commands within the Soul will always be followed, for the Lord of your Being is responsive to you now, and not a dark and mysterious element called the "subconscious" or alter-ego.

This re-programming of the Soul takes patient practice and dedication, which is equated on this plane to effort. That is because everyone thinks that Life should be easy—and so it should. But who and what defines easy? You must learn to make your own definitions for *your* design of Life. The re-programming also requires consistency, but you will find that you can command the Soul to your specifications. After all, it's a servant unto you not a dictator. Take the effort to listen to your Soul, to work *with* it. Then the limited ego is being confronted and made an integral part of the divine whole Self. You are putting yourself back together again to operate as a unity, a Oneness, a complete God. : *Unlimited Ego.*

This feeling that troubled you so before, perhaps it is being felt acutely by someone around you, someone you Love who is far away, or someone you don't even know. In your grander understanding of it through contemplation you'll discover that you are constantly perceiving the emotions and Thoughts of all those around you, and so it becomes a part of you as you feel it. But as you open up to the God of your Being and the

God in all peoples and things, you're not affected so painfully or adversely anymore. The unknowing is the greatest pain and greatest fear.

Other Gods all around you are in a swamp of Thoughts and emotions that they do not confront or allow, and they do not realize how powerfully they affect you and everyone nearby, for Thoughts are the same as actions. They're subtle and quick and less understood on this plane of heavy sensation, for that is the accustomed mode here.

Honor

I have come to a great peace within my Being concerning all people, and it is called Honor. In learning to honor my own emotions I have learned to honor the feelings of others. When I relinquish the expectations of how others should act or re-act, feel or see things, or how I want them to see *me*, then I can honor them for what they do feel. Then I honor people simply for being whatever they are. This is respect and recognition of the God in ALL peoples. Then the perfection realized within my own Being is readily seen reflected back to me through all else.

By constantly seeing the God (good) in my own emotions I am able to see it clearly in all things. As I *AM* the Father and experience everything through His Eye, which is the God of my Being, all that seemed before to be without or apart from me, I now see sweetly and Lovingly as being within myself. The irritations and judgments that were harbored in my emotions, now I simply place an individual in my Soul and see them as a part of me. Then these feelings melt away and a great calm consumes me. This is my realized truth:

Whatever one expresses, he does so out of knowingness, for it comes from feelings, and that is all that knowingness is.

I have learned to honor and respect the knowingness of all peoples in this way. It derives from their feelings, and this is their truth.

This receivership simply means openness to any emotion, to all Thoughts, without automatically applying a label. All things are the Father and no thing can harm you. If you are in perfect receivership it simply flows in and is noted, felt, recorded and acknowledged, then flows on, leaving you wiser and stronger for the experience.

This is also a detachment from the thick of things, that is, from the illusions of the power that social behavior and "conditions" seem to dictate to Man.

If you were to visualize yourself suddenly out of your body and in a vortex of pure Thought, you'd have the feelings and Thoughts that seem so confusing and complex, but you'd have no mass structure to base comparisons upon which only limit and cloister your thinking. You'd have no society and no expectations to consider above yourself, no walls to define and no relationships to obligate you. All that you'd be is pure and simple *emotion*. Ponder this. When a situation becomes difficult to bear, close your eyes for a few moments and visualize yourself high above the earth, with only the Thought, only your pure emotion. Then the stakes aren't so high, the air becomes less oppressive. Hover over the earth for a few centuries and just watch. The same entities return to the same families and lovers, express the same tyranny and the same enslavement over and over again. Life doesn't end with the intensity of emotion, it becomes *richer*. Then, if you wish to struggle through things, return to the earth, but you'll have a lighter perspective on Life and the struggle becomes humorous, a joke!

I have enjoyed watching myself wiggle through incidents which I know I created myself, and instead of being weighed down by them I've learned to appreciate the gains I make through them. Life is a joy when you are aware that the Father lives through you.

*   *   *

Beloved Father, O Lord of my Is-ness,
I feel you to the depths of my openness
to the heights of my receivership of Emotion
of the Thought Divine.
Blessed feelings, O Spirit of my Being,
Come Quicken my Soul to an understanding of all
    that
I BE, of all that
I *feel*.

     Suddenly I am not alone. I am in a community of
Souls, other Gods, other Beings. All have emotions
running the length and breadth of our experience
into the collective expression that we BE, moment
to moment.

Suddenly my peace is jolted, I am not feeling that
which I have designed for myself, that which I
choose to feel. My perception opens and I am
feeling THEIR feelings, for I am open to the Soul of

others even as I am open in receivership to the
Thoughts of the God I Am.
Awkward, off balance, I struggle to be ME, to keep
my joy in spite of the confusion. I feel my feelings,
and do not insist on understanding them.

Bless you beloved friends, brothers, sisters,
I Love you truly.
We share our feelings, communing gently, and live
in peace together for a time.

Now I am alone again.
Blessed Father come forth from within me to
manifest a clear understanding of my moment of
experience with others in their wonder, in their
feelings and choices.

AH! I see it now!
It is Emotion Divine!
It is receivership to *all* that surrounds me that
brings this sharing, this closeness to the conditions
of others.
It is passed now, but lingers in the memory as a
triumph of the non-judgment of my feelings.
O Oneness with all that IS in Life,
my Kingdom, O Blessed Father.

O Lord of my Being, see the moment, the precious
NOW.

I am not lost, I am not less for my experience, nay
I AM greater!
I have added to my awareness of these beautiful
Gods and so of myself. Let me be ever open to the
River of Emotion, of the Father that is within me.

ALL emotions are God.
ALL peoples are God.
ALL experience shines forth from my singular
perspective of the Father which is LIFE. Let me
live the joy that bubbles up from my Soul, O Lord,
O servant divine.
Let me rejoice in the Father in ALL THINGS.
Let me be a reflection of Him in all that I see and
hear, feel and know.

Beloved Father, my
Source, my
Friend, my Self,
Let my flesh reflect your highest ideal.

I AM the Christ, the
Is-ness, the
Perfect Son of You, my most perfect Father, which
IS the spark of Life within me.

*   *   *

Once you have perceived a Thought and pondered its nature in regards to you, you've opened the doors for yet a grander perspective of this self same Thought to be perceived, and for an entire spectrum of other Thoughts to enter also. This brings more feeling, more awareness in the moments to follow. Always this is the way. Always we are expanding and growing even if we aren't aware or willing, for this is the nature of the Father.

To open yourself to all emotions is the way of working *with* the Source and living in the flow of the God of your Being. If it doesn't appear to work 100% the first time you test this out, don't be discouraged and stop. If you've "tried" it you've *done* it, for in the Lord God of your Being there is no "trying". All that you feel or imagine you *become*, however subtly. Be patient. It may take a while for you to fully accept that this is even possible let alone master it. If there is a bit of doubt or disbelief then the Soul, and most certainly the alter-ego, will be aware of it. This dilutes your power over fears and anxieties.

You've spent years and even lifetimes programming these things in. To release them takes patience and *reverence* of Self. Love is always the best ally. When you bless these emotions and Love them truly (for now you understand them better and have grown from the expression of them) and Love yourself unconditionally, you relax in your own Being and find inner peace. This of course signals the Being to open more and show you more of yourself to experience and to Love.

This is unconditional Love.

Unconditional Love

The essence of unconditional Love is unlimited and unconditional Love of Self. To Love Self in ALL moments, regardless of their content and regardless of the emotion, is to be in unconditional union with the Father. This displays to the Soul that ALL things are now recognized as the Father. Unconditional Love is standing in complete and utter receivership in the Ocean of Thought.

In a moment of discomfort or disagreement, to Love Self truly is not to define one's Self through these feelings. Not to define Self through *any* situation or through any attitude of another is to unlimit Self and demonstrate non-judgment. Then a glorious inner peace is acquired which is a loftier perspective. This demonstrates itself as understanding and compassion for the very things which attempt so vigorously to define and limit Self. It brings understanding and great compassion for the inner workings of your alter-ego, and for the outward manifestation of the expectations of others.

To come to an awareness and Love of what IS and relinquish expectations of what "should be" or what you "should feel," this is profound wisdom. Expectations are based on a limited view, a speculation or theorem. That which IS, as seen and felt in a moment in its full bloom, floats gently into the consciousness as a grand and unique commodity brought forth into greater Life through complete acceptance and Love of what IS. This is God realized.

Then the expression of Love for others, and compassion—which is only a moment of understanding their view and Loving them for it—issues forth of itself naturally and comfortably from within the Being. Then the desire is manifest which has the possibility of being without expectations: to *share* Self, not affirm and validate Self.

Unconditional Love of Self dissolves the needs for conditions of a specific nature and displays uncondition as the mode: Oneness and Joy in ALL feelings, in ALL moments and with ALL peoples. This is a sublime expression of Self, for it demonstrates *to Self* that no thing, entity, emotion or situation can alter Self or minimize it in any way.

All experiences add to Self in an ever-broadening *perspective* on the flow called Life. Love which is termed "blind" is based on the true nature of Love, blindness denoting a lack of concern (judgment) for the comparative value of that which is being Loved. This "blind" Love is all-knowing, all-perspective, all *essence to essence*, all GOD.

To Love unconditionally all emotions and all Thoughts is not to pretend that they are all joyful or easy. They may not be a part of that which you would design for your kingdom. But to Love them is to conquer, and this will encompass them in a perspective which stems from the *conclusive knowingness* that these incidents, these feelings are no longer ruling you, rather you are in control of them. You can see them in any light that you have the capacity to. Know that the kingdom of Heaven is right within you. In the experiences that you gain here on this plane of comparison and illusion, and in your demonstration of your feelings, you are becoming *wisdom*.

The awareness begins: In all your moments you are becoming more of you. In all your emotions you are *feeling*. Were the feeling to cease you would cease. To embrace your emotions is to recognize that they are what you are. Love of *you* is unconditional Love of the Father, who is conditionless, egoless, limitless, judgeless. Thus, you *become* the Father when you Love YOU.

Whatever you are feeling will expand you into more expression of yourself, which is more of the Father *realized* within your Being. This brings the understanding into an arena wherein you can see ALL LIFE within YOU. You are large enough, grand enough, GOD enough to contain *ALL* of it, yea even to Love all of it, for it is the Father-God which *IS* you.

*   *   *

Karma

Forgiveness of Self is an immediate release from all so-called "negative" influences in a splendid moment. It is forgiving yourself for all that you have limited and all that you have feared in yourself and in your Life. You are the only one that has ever been in possession of you. You have only yourself to release yourself from.

Many are concerned with something called karma—which only means balance—and its supposed "laws" and effects on their lives. Karma exists only in the man who believes in it, and it is spawned into great power through the feelings of guilt. Without guilt, karma would not be. Its "laws" are not set forth to Mankind from the outside or "above." They were invented by Man in ignorance of his *divine* origin. The Father did not create karma, nor does He bring it down on any Man. The Supreme Life Force and Directive Principle is not a judge. Only Man, who judges *all things* and calls one action or Thought right and another wrong, could create "laws" to justify one thing and restrict or ban another. That laws exist in the Mind of the Source is a great fallacy. The balancing occurs within the feelings within each Man, each God, in a moment to moment response-ability to Self. God-realized Man does not live by laws, he lives by FEELINGS.

All things are God, and all actions Thoughts and words are of God. To separate one thing as divine and another as less, is to limit and define the Father. And to limit yourself to that which another has set himself over you to dictate what is good for you and what is not, is to live another's Thought of Life and not your own. To be *your Thought* of you always is simply to act, speak and *think* that which makes *you* feel good. If another doesn't approve, that is his to reckon. If he attempts to enslave you to his way of thinking and living and expressing, he is being enslaved by the mass thinking, or by someone to whom he gives undeserved authority, and he is not even free within his own Being to even suggest how you should or should not think or express.

You will balance within yourself all the feelings which manifest to you—you always have. And if there is a question, ask your own Spirit, the God within you. That entity within will never judge you or limit you in any way. That entity will lead you into JOY.

*   *   *

I am asked: how can I condone the violence of either a verbal or physical nature that exists so openly on this plane? I do not condone, nor do I judge my brother who is the perpetrator of such acts. To judge him would be to compare and to separate him from myself and I would never do that. I *AM* the Father. I *AM* my brethren, *all* of them without condition. I Love this Man who does these things, for he is also God. I see it readily in him even when no others will take the pains to set their sights above the obvious. To judge these actions and situations is to give energy to the very thing that causes the situation to occur in the first place: the *attitude*.

When one Man strikes his brother, all are quick to lay siege to him *in their Thoughts*. And so, in their judgment and ensuing emotion they strike *him* with mental violence which is no less severe. This adds a momentum and confusion to the act, and in a high state of emotion it is not perceived how the victim of this time was once the assailant on the other in a previous lifetime. Or that the victim feared its occurrence for such a time and intensity in the Thought of it, that he literally drew it to himself. Fear is the great amplifier of emotion, and draws the feared thing more quickly and intensely into a fruition on this plane, in three-dimensional form or mass or action. To feel these acts of violence, or to hold them in your Thoughts, is to make them a part of your own kingdom, your Life. That is the way it is:

What you contemplate you become.

Your Thoughts are powerful things. To learn not to judge them is to accept your feelings without labeling them good or bad, without fearing them or allowing them to define you. You can feel anger in a moment; that doesn't mean that you're an angry God. You are simply a God expressing an emotion, but you are still a God.

Bless all that are involved in these actions and situations, Love them all, and this assists the swifter reckoning of the situation and gives your energy (Thought) to an ideal, that it will be finished and not laid away in the feelings—the Soul—only to occur again in yet another time.

Thought is the generator of all your realities, your kingdom of the NOW, and collectively your Thoughts draw unto you the NOWs of the future. The result of all actions and Thoughts is not karma, but rather the *FEELINGS* that you have, that you carry around, that you ARE. Feelings is what we *are*.

The feelings you have about you will always lead you to the best choices in all your moments. When you are functioning in and of, by and through YOU, all will be right in your kingdom. Of course this requires that you take full responsibility for yourself and all that you are. This is frightening to some, but it is the greatest JOY I can assure you, for this is freedom. Then you become a sovereign Being and utterly free. Then your reasoning becomes refined and your thinking clear, and you never have to depend on anyone or anything for your happiness or livelihood, or for your BEING which is immanent.

Anything you wish to know is right there closer than your breath in the Ocean of consciousness. Anything you desire is yours the moment you conceive of it and stand in complete receivership of it. This means being willing to accept all that the Source delivers, and on the terms through which it comes. Always your desires will manifest, all of them, but *in the emotion*. Often the wills of others are involved and a desire is fulfilled in an unexpected course of events. This is because of expectations and "pictures" that are held in your mind of how things "should be." To manifest quickly, become flexible enough to recognize the emotional value of a desire, and its equivalent feeling at its fulfillment within your Being, in whatever form it arrives.

This entails letting go of some of the "pictures" you might have, for your Spirit will surprise you in the events and emotions that manifest. All your Thoughts will manifest, be they dreads or desires; your Spirit does not judge them, it simply brings them to you that you can see them, feel and understand them, and move on into the next moment.

All your manifestations occur in feelings, but not always in a three-dimensional understanding. Peace is derived when you see and realize that no feeling or Thought that manifests either inwardly or outwardly can alter or threaten you. All add to your collective understanding.

As you have undoubtedly noticed I use the word *feelings* more than frequently. I will explain why this is the crux of things. When an entity passes from this plane, whether it is to ascend the body into the seventh, or to allow the body to die and pass to the plane which is aligned with his attitude collective understanding, all that the entity takes with him in the equivalent of the experiences gained here, is *emotions*.

The sum total of all that you are and will be and have been, on this or any other plane of expression, be it right or wrong, famous or neglected, good or bad, the result of all of this in your Life into forever, is feelings. It is your perception of you, of the Father and the nature of Life, which determines to which plane or Heaven you will pass. When you struggle to gain wealth, it is for the feelings that this experience will bring. When you are desirous of Love and fame, it is for the wonderful feelings that you derive in the center of your Being. All of Life on this illusionary plane of mass and matter exists that you might learn and become, grow and teach you, and experience all of this through the emotions that this fabric of form and its consciousness brings.

And why are we here at all? It is to have joy. That is all that the Father-Principle desires for any of us. And WHAT IS JOY? I will share with you a perspective on joy by an entity that I Love beyond expression:

"Joy is the freedom of movement, without interruption. It is the freedom of expression, without judgment. It is the freedom of Being, without guilt. Joy is the sublime movement of Self, allowed."

Joy allows all of Life to be felt, to be expressed, and to be cherished, whatever it brings in the next moment.

Seven Heavens/Seven Seals

In the seven chakras it is the raising of the shakti, or energy, up through the body which awakens and enlarges these ductless glands or seals. The first of these is in the genitals. It is aligned with this plane, this Heaven which is the first of the seven planes, and this chakra or seal was created to insure the procreation of Mankind on this plane. This allows Gods to continue to return here in bodies, that they will be created and our expression in mass will continue. The greatest energy of all was placed here in the loins and womb of Man. It contains the blueprint of the Thought that is the essence of Man on this plane.

Each cell of your wondrous body is based on a spark of light-synthesis. Each cell contains its own Soul, its own Life Force. This is the God within you. This is why the death of the body is so painful and traumatic, for when the Spirit gathers to it the Soul and departs, it leaves behind a part of itself in this cellular Life Force. The body continues to produce new cells and rebuild itself even after death. Bodies that have been exhumed months and years after burial are found to have fingernails and hair that has grown six or more inches. This Life Force does not leave the body completely for many years.

The second seal is located in the lower abdomen, just above the genitals, and is aligned with pain and fear. When an entity expresses predominantly into pain or fear, this is the seat of his perception of Self, and of Life. When this entity passes, the Spirit collects the Soul and goes to the second plane. There, this God will learn of pain and fear in a pure emotion.

The third seal is in the solar plexus region of the body and is the seal of power. Those who enslave others to their attitudes and modes of behavior, who insist that things must be seen or done in *their* way, these entities when they pass this plane go to the third. Also those who have continually been enslaved, because they have allowed it to occur, and aren't happy unless someone else is taking responsibility, these pass also to the third. There they will experience power and its consequences until they have had their fill.

Tyrants are aligned with the third. This is a new age, however, and soon the tyrants and enslavers will be no more on the earth. It is becoming a paradise.

The fourth Heaven is that of Love, but unexpressed. Its seal is in the chest cavity next to the heart wherein lies the Soul. It is the predominating seal for those entities who feel Love, who feel deeply their emotions but do not express them. On the fourth plane they learn of Love and its importance in expression of emotion.

The fifth is a paradise. All that is conceived and desired comes forth immediately into manifestation. It comes not into form, rather into light, into Thought in its realized emotion. The fifth is aligned with Love that is known and expressed. Its seal is in the throat, and this is the seal of expression and of teaching.

Those who express on the fifth are aware of God, to be on the fifth is to know God. Many entities pass to the fifth and remain for aeons, for once in paradise they forget that there is anything better. All is light and sound and a myriad of colors on the fifth. All the colors on the first plane are as but *one hue* on the fifth.

The sixth Heaven. Seeing God in all things. Located in the pineal gland at the base of the brain, this seal is sometimes called the "third eye," which represents "psychic" abilities and etheric vision, the ability to perceive what is invisible, or that which surrounds the mass and matter of this plane. This is the plane of contemplative Thought and it is the door to the seventh.

When an entity sees clearly the Father-Principle in all that IS and Loves and expresses that vision, that entity is expressing on the sixth. Many spend a life-time perfecting their vision and attempting to master their Thoughts. Yet they do not recognize their very flesh as the divine vehicle which will take them into the seventh. They do not conceive of the potentially unlimited counterpart to the nearly unlimited vision which many of them acquire. They starve the body and leave it for lengthy periods of time in order to grasp the feeling of Is-ness, of un-limited freedom. But they do not realize that this can be attained and *lived here*, on this plane. Then, at a chosen time, which many of them announce and gather followers around to witness, they leave the body for the last time and allow it to die, that the consciousness is at last freed from this plane of limitation and comparison. These entities pass to the sixth, which is actually the seventh, save that there is no vehicle for expression should they ever desire to return to this plane.

This may seem to be a foolish desire, but when the body is taken up *with* the Spirit consciousness, that entity is free to come and go as he pleases. He may also travel to other worlds and universes and express through form there, where form is the mode. Then he is One with all planes, and there is no thing of any and all of the universes that is out of his reach. There is, after all, much to be enjoyed on the first. It is Heaven also.

The pituitary is the master gland, the seventh seal. When this seal opens it activates the entirety of the brain into alignment with the highest and subtlest vibrations of Thought. The sixth and seventh chakras together are actually the crown, for their functions are complementary, and in union they are the greatest seals, allowing the perception to be ever expansive with each moment and each new Thought.

While the pituitary regulates the reception of Thought, the pineal is concerned with the transmission of these heightened physical vibrations and images which come from the Soul as feelings, into the auric structure, the Spirit. As this occurs the message is sent out into the universe and draws to itself greater momentum, and acts as an electro-magnet as all Thoughts relative to this feeling and awareness of heightened emotion and vibration are drawn back to you. Thus the truth of the saying, "*you are what you think*." You are what you *feel*.

The pineal is located on top of the medulla oblongata. It is the sixth center, which when opened allows the impulses from the Soul to create images within the brain that the memory can be visualized, and perceptions (which come from feelings) can be recognized as images. This is "clairvoyance" or clear seeing, and it occurs as the pineal opens.

The pituitary is forward and above the brow, behind the center of the forehead. The two together acitivate the greater highway of Thought into light and into electrical impulses which is the central nervous system. As this occurs greater and greater, the body raises in its vibrations higher and higher until one day, in a moment of utter peace and simple Beingness, the Thought enters, "I Am lifted," and the body simply returns to Light/Spirit/ Thought. This is ascension pure and simple.

Of the seven seals, they operate in unison and in a flow of energy throughout the body. To isolate your thinking on one or two is to inhibit the flow. I perceive the entire body as one stream of light energy with all the seals pulsing in unison. There are also many more centers that are minor chakras located in the hands and feet, torso, shoulders, legs and arms. The importance of the seven major seals is their alignment with the different planes of expression or attitude.

It is possible to be aligned with any plane or seal predominantly and also to express through all the others at various times. For example, one who is expressing primarily on the fifth, can also express through the first, in sexual intercourse, through the sixth by recognizing God in a moment of contemplation, or through the seventh. Expressing on the seventh is *BEING* God.

Blessings

The blessings that you speak forth on yourself, your friend, your car or a feeling that you have, this is righteous power and issues forth from the third seal. When you bless some thing or some one, you are standing forth in your power to arrange Thought into your design, that is to do your bidding. Ramtha says that a blessing is as a great sword of light that comes forth from the solar plexus and cuts through the fears and confusions of limited thinking. It is power of Thought. To bless yourself signals to the Soul that you Love and align Self with the Father-God within you.

I have seen the power of blessings on several occasions, and all who practice this have wonderful stories to tell of incidents that are transformed from disaster and misfortune, into lessons of joy and Loving communication between people.

My friend Linda is a nurse. She deals with many cancer patients and administers medication intravenously. She has seen patients who were "impossible" to calm or even speak to, become suddenly cooperative and quiet. Each time she enters a room to give treatment she blesses everyone involved, including the other nurses and staff, and sees the God in the patient and in all things concerning the situation. When you look inside, to the God within someone, you'll find that things are simpler, sweeter, and harmony is given a chance to ring out among people. It is the God in one Man giving the signal to the God of another that he has a "blank check" to be or feel, act or speak however he chooses, and to know that he will not be judged or squelched. This is Loving in freedom.

Among strangers and in potentially difficult situations, the blessing is a peacemaker. It is your opportunity to demonstrate to Self *continually* that you are now greater than the obstacles which confront and attempt to define you. This is righteous (right-use-of) power.

My friend Linda has found that her work as a nurse is augmented tremendously, for in each instance when she blesses someone, their Spirit responds, and in a greater capacity for allowing themselves to heal themselves, her caring and Love of people is given a chance to be seen. Even when the person isn't outwardly aware of what's happening to them, the Spirit knows and responds to her touch.

Hierarchy

And what of power? What of the control that so many fear or surrender to as being wielded upon them from without? It is a NO THING. It does not exist.

Hierarchy, as it is defined, comes from the Greek word "hierarchia," which means "power or rule of a hierarch," which comes from the "hieros: sacred" and "archein: to rule or lead." Thus it has come to mean the ruler or leader of a religious group or society.

As the early religions developed, the problem of controlling and predicting or, as the leaders will tell us, "directing" great numbers of people arose. The truth is, one took it upon himself to dictate to the others what was "holy," which was correct in the eyes of God, and what was evil or wrong. Thus the concept arose and was worshipped that one action or practice could be against or separate from the Father—who is *ALL LIFE*—while another was in

117

greater accord. This is the blasphemy that has frag-mented Mankind and enslaved him to dogma and religious rule for aeons. It is time that it is finished, for Man is becoming aware of his divinity and his birthright, which is Holy in *all places* and things, and One with the Father-Source in *all moments*.

In order for a hierarchy even to be it is necessary to presume that a ruler is needed. It is also neces-sary to conjecture that in the realms of the Father-Mother Principle a graduated scale of power and order exists. This is not the case. For if it were, the Father would be qualitative principle, and a judge against and unto Himself. This is most assuredly not so, for if the Father were to judge Himself, all Life as it is would cease, and the expansive move-ment which is the essence of Life would not BE.

The Father is an equananimous Life Force given freely to all who will stand forth in receiver-ship of it. In the realm of Spirit there is no graduated scale of power, with one entity over another. There is *no measure* of existence or ability or power in the Mind of God, for all entities have been given these things equally and conclusively within their own Beings, though most on this plane do not take them unto their own.

On this plane of limited consciousness-awareness, Life is continually measured. One perception is always being compared to another as having more or less validity. That is because the mass view here and its fickle fashion is the basis and controlling factor in how the infinity of the all-consuming Principle of Life is perceived. This fashion and mass consciousness has the awesome power—which you give it—of influencing all your decisions.

If the Father were an individual entity or view, then a hierarchy would follow naturally, for then all would be following after this one ideal which would set a precedent for all others. But this is not the case.

The Principle is no singular movement or ego-perspective (do you really think that a singular God created all this?). The Principle is the plural movement, which is the Thought-synthesis behind all Life. The Father is the ALL-in-ALL. To attempt to define God according to the limited concepts of this plane is to create a God in *Man's image*, and force the infinite and all-consuming, all-encompassing Directive Intelligence into the pint container of Man's understanding.

The only singular example of the Father, complete in and of its own Being, is *YOU*, and you are already the perfect ideal *for* you.

When Man leaves this plane as God to begin a new adventure on the seventh, it is with the understanding that ALL MEN are held *equally* in the Mind of the Father. All actions and expressions are of divine sovereignty, and on the seventh there is no measure. It is only Man in his cloistered view which allows one mode to *appear* greater or lesser. Entities who are no more bound by this plane have no desire to control or rule here, for they have demonstrated that anything they desire to obtain or become is taken right from within their own Thought. And the emotion and fulfillment IS the moment of experiencing it. And to control the Thoughts and destinies of other Gods? To what purpose when they themselves are already all things, all feelings conclusively within their own Thought?

You cannot enslave another God. You can possibly take all knowingness away and leave him with superstition and dogmatic rule, but even then he will do as he pleases. This is obvious.

There are many entities from other universes and planes, other dimensions, which live right within our own. They are benevolent guides because of their Loving Thoughts, and a few are powerful organizers, for they have a concern for this plane and an understanding as to what is needed here for ALL to acquire the awareness and freedom to become *complete God* in their individualized attitude of Self. They are not in control of anyone for what would they do with you once they had you? They are busy living for themselves, but they are great Lovers of your Being and a blessing to be sure.

And many on this plane speak of the Christ Consciousness, or "Cosmic Energy," or another "energy," which is to descend from the Heavens to enlighten this plane of helpless creatures. The only energy and consciousness that is of any consequence to anyone in raising themselves to an awareness of higher levels of Thought and perception, is the energy that is right within each individual. *This* is the Christ energy. This is the Source of all knowingness and light.

All that energy is, is Thought. The only way to partake of that energy is to receive the Thought and *feel* its relationship to your own Life, your own perception of who you BE. No "energy" from without will matter until it is felt and understood in its vibrational frequency. This is accomplished only by *becoming* the very Thought or energy which is sent from another plane of understanding of God. Then the energy is aligned with the *receiver* in his own capacity to understand, and his perception grows accordingly. Then the sender and the receiver are One. The receiver becomes the Source of energy *for himself,* for now he has *felt* it and can draw it from within his Soul at any time he desires.

Thus you begin to see that no outside force or energy or directive is necessary. You find yourself privy to the same Ocean of Thought, the same Peace, Joy and Totality of Expression as any other Christ, any God of *ANY* dimension, plane, universe or understanding.

*   *   *   *

And so of hierarchy, it exists *not.* It is the concept of an enslaved and ignorant people who will depend on a "miracle" to descend on them from the Heavens to "save" them at some specula-tive future, and so do not live NOW, until they realize that the Father-God is they themselves.

Only each Man, each God himself can rescue his own individual attitude from the enslavement of the mass view, which would have him always limited and thus predictable, for then he can be controlled. To look to hierarchy is to look outside for the simple essence, which is power, which has been *within* all along.

*   *   *   *

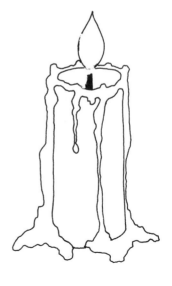

I have mentioned the assistance that I've received from the Ram. In his unspeakable Love and constant example he has taught me how to reason these things for myself. I have learned from entities all around, seen and unseen. I have learned each day from the beautiful Gods that I live with, and Gods that I meet on the street, in the supermarket, and in their labors. I learn something grand and new in each moment of my existence, for I Am GOD, I AM LIFE.

For me being God means that the learning never ends. It means becoming a child again and opening up to the abundance of Life that teems all around. It means dropping the masks of maturity and somber composure that are too often associated with "spirituality." What *isn't* spiritual?

To be delighted in a ray of sunshine, enough that I would scream with pleasure and run to have

my face in it. To forget all that is weighing in regards to some thing or another in order to feel the
rain on my cheeks and head—to really *feel* it. To
smell the blossoms of a grand fruit tree and enjoy
the beauty of the day that surrounds.

Walking down a country road or on a city street
is a deliciously lush and lusty experience when you
feel the Life Force pulsating, resonating in every
molecule of each tree, wind, cloud, drop of dew,
dust, flower and Man that you encounter. It fills my
senses to their capacity and makes me feel as
though I'll burst! It opens the very cells of the body
to receive *more* feeling, more *Life*. This has been
my greatest teacher: LIFE. Being God means Being
Life.

I say that a "new age" has begun. It is the Age
of Spirit, the Age of God. I have also stated that this
plane is becoming a paradise. And what of the
doomsday prophets? Do not fear them, they are
gross enslavers. They wish to embroil you in the
same limited thinking which has inhibited and in-
timidated Mankind for ages. *IT IS FINISHED.*

The prophets of doom will fall at their own
hands. They will all experience their predicted
armageddon, but in a place and time when it will
suit their collective will. And innocent victims? There

will be *NONE.* Those who fear damnation and destruction will have it, along with those who prophesy it. But they will be a bit disappointed in one respect, for the gentle bird and blossom of this earth will live on forever. And any and all who wish to partake in the glorifying and heightening of this plane will have every opportunity to do so in the days and years to come. At this very moment the light of this plane grows stronger. The electro-magnetic field of the planet itself is being raised to a grander and higher pulse and rhythm. This transformation has already begun, and you will see a paradise of beauty and peace unfold.

*   *   *   *

Ramtha taught me to contemplate my own Being, to become my own ideal to myself. I have taught me to see myself in all things. This is my ideal: When all that is without is recognized and seen as Self, God is expressing sublimely within and through you. Then you are Loving you, and the Supreme Life Force within each cell quickens and intensifies in its vibration, and the molecules within each cell are transfigured into light, and the body ascends.

Of all that I have written, the greatest that I would have you ponder, is how to *LOVE YOU.* I Love you profoundly, and bless you from the Lord God of my Being to the Lord God of your wondrous and glorious Being!

Life flows on, it is the only absolute there IS, and we flow with it evenly and gracefully by being at Peace within.

Be *joyful* always in your astounding beauty.

Simply *BE*.

*   *   *

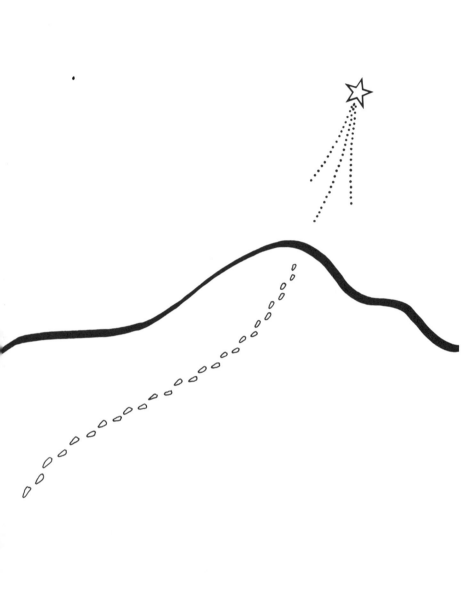

·